"Samantha has an amazing ability to take someone through the process of how they can tune into their story, help them understand their why, help them close the gap of where they are and where they want to be."

Gina B. | Transformation Coach

Connect with Samantha at

https://www.findyourcreativestrategy.com
www.instagram.com/fiercelycreate
www.facebook.com/fiercelycreate
www.pinterest.ca/fiercelycreate

Blogfluent

Laying the Foundation for Your Successful Blog

By Samantha Laycock

Edited by Curt Casetta

Published by Trenton House Publishing, West Bend, WI
TrentonHousePublishing.com
TrentonHousePublishing@gmail.com
Twitter: @trentonhouseWI

BLOGFLUENT

Laying the Foundation For Your Successful Blog

BY SAMANTHA LAYCOCK

Dedicated to

my husband, Richard, who
showed me that I was worthy of
love before I could love myself,
and to my children,
Quinton, Anneleise, and Iliza,
who remind me every day to
laugh, be silly and embrace
who I am in the moment.

Table of Contents

Prologue

My journey

I sat in front of my old Apple desktop computer, a computer that we bought second-hand just so we had one. That was the day my life changed. I had no idea what I was doing. I had never even considered starting a blog before but I was at the point in my life I was willing to try everything and anything to just start feeling better about who I was.

You see, I couldn't even look at myself in the mirror. I hated my reflection and everything about me. I should have been happy with my life. In 2014, I was a mom to two beautiful children, a wife to the man I loved (and still do) and we had just moved across Canada to start a new chapter in our lives.

Money was tight but we had never been happier. Things were beginning to look up and I felt the same then as I did when I was first accepted into university as a senior in high school. As if the world was opening up for me and I could do anything and everything that I wanted to.

There was one big piece of me that was blocking all that happiness and all that growth for me. My past.

It was keeping me feeling small and incomplete.
It was keeping me unsatisfied in my life.
It was keeping me in the self-hatred that I had been carrying around for years.

My past was my undoing. Or so I thought. I thought to truly be happy in life, we just had to move on from our past. Don't think about it. Just keep moving forward.

But the real truth is…

In order to truly move forward, we need to look at our past. We need to examine it. We need to give it love. We need to embrace it. We need to own it.

And so, I sat in front of that computer screen with a blinking cursor, and I knew what I needed to do. I began to type.

It was inside me all along. It was waiting for permission to come out. It had been screaming at me for years to release it and allow the healing journey to begin, but I just wasn't ready *until* that day.

That day in October, when a computer became my best friend, my safe place. A way for me to release the hurt, the fear, the doubt and the secret that I had been holding onto for so many years. I began to write my story. I began to rewrite my future. I began to acknowledge, accept, and believe that there was power in my past. That there was even a way for me to use my past to begin to change my future.

That day in October shifted who I thought I was and who I thought I was becoming. It reminded me of who I truly was.

That day in October, I stepped into my power and now I am here to help show you how to step into yours.

In order to truly move forward,
we need to look at our past.
We need to examine it.
We need to give it love.
We need to embrace it.
We need to own it.

Preface

Why learn from me?

There are so many experts out there nowadays, and you have access to an unlimited amount of them with technology. So, why me?

Every time I talk about blogging and sharing your story, I get these little flutters in my heart. These flutters remind me that I am doing what I am supposed to be doing. That I am right where I am meant to be.

Through years of blogging. Through countless hours of spending my time learning how to blog, I am here today, writing this book for you.

You don't need to do the countless hours on YouTube.
You don't need to download every piece of free content that you can find.
You don't need to learn how to blog on your own.

I have done the work for you. I am here today because of the passion that teaching women how to harness the power of their words through blogging brings me.

I may not be the best out there and this isn't a "dis" to me. I pride myself on always learning, always moving forward, and when I think that I am the best, that ends, and I don't want it to. I want to push myself to be better than I was yesterday.

Through the support of amazing friends and family. Through the support of women who trusted me enough to help them with this piece of their life. I am here to help you walk through the blogging process with confidence. When you bring confidence into your blogging, your readers and your followers will know.

Thank you for being here and being another one of these women who is supporting me. A woman who reminds me every single day why I am doing the work that I am doing. A woman who is ready to learn how to blog without confusion and being overwhelmed.

When you bring confidence into your blogging, your readers and your followers will know.

Chapter 1

Why blogging?

You're reading this for a reason. I mean, the title of this book is called *Laying the Foundation for Your Successful Blog*. Clearly, you know you want to blog, but you may be confused about how to actually begin. So here you are. No need to search any longer for information on how to start a blog.

I was once where you are right now. I didn't have the slightest clue how to blog. Being the woman that I am, I jumped–with both feet. I have a tendency to just start things I am passionate about. I know if I allow my logical brain to kick in, I won't start, and I will talk myself out of it. And that's how I started blogging.

Blogging felt safe. A way to feel anonymous while sharing my deep, dark secrets with the world. A way to blend in while standing out. A way to give myself a purpose without making it all about me.

Blogging was a way for me to write. A passion that I've had since grade 5, when a teacher showed me that writing can be incredibly healing. I remember writing a letter to my grandfather that year. We were incredibly close, and losing him without being allowed to say goodbye, crushed me. I didn't know how to process the emotions in a way that would make sense. I needed a way to get all of the thoughts out of my head. That letter went into his casket with him. I felt as if he knew everything that I had written in that letter. My pain didn't disappear, but my ability to cope with the grief was manageable.

Blogging was sold to me as an online journal and that no one would read what I was going to write anyway. Now that I think about it, it probably wasn't the greatest selling point, but it was EXACTLY what I needed to hear at that moment in my life. I needed to know I could pour my heart and soul onto a page and risk no judgement from others.

I now know there are people that will hear and read my words. There are people reading my words the instant I hit publish. And, by then, it's too late to turn around. One of the biggest lessons I learned through blogging is that my past is someone else's current reality. This gives my story, my past, meaning.

How powerful is that?

So why blogging?

You are giving someone out there a voice.

You are giving yourself a way to heal.
You are teaching the world your passion.

There are roughly 500 million blogs in the world.

500 MILLION.

Let that number sink in for a minute.

500 million people are writing their stories, showcasing their passions, and showing the world that words can change the world. You, along with 500 million people, are connecting strangers and leaving a legacy for your children and grandchildren to read.

So why choose to blog?

It's a way to reach new people.
It's a way to share your knowledge.
It's a way to make a positive impact in the world.

Blogging is a simple way to get your name out there and start to showcase your expertise in whichever niche you choose. You may be laughing right now after reading that sentence.

"Expert?! Ha. I'm no expert in anything."

The thing is, you are an expert. You have knowledge. You have a unique perspective that no one else has. This makes you an expert. No one else can be an expert on your life. Only you can be.

Blogging allows you to control the content you put out into the world and to attract your ideal readers to your website. Blogging is a simple tool to teach and connect all at once.

The common misconception is that blogging is just about writing content and putting it on a website. As you'll discover, blogging is much more than that. To truly succeed at blogging, you need to have a plan and you need to lay down a foundation that will help you to continue to grow and expand.

Blogging has multiple moving pieces. When one of those pieces is off or missing, it affects the whole process. This book will guide you to learn what you need to succeed in blogging and how to create a blog that is going to last for years and years.

If you're ready to learn how to create a foundation that will help you build a successful blog, then jump in—with both feet—and begin your journey to blogging.

You have knowledge. You have a unique perspective that no one else has. This makes you an expert.

Chapter 2

Beginning with the why

I start in the same place with EVERY client that I work with. It doesn't matter if they already have a blog or if they're just beginning to think about starting a blog. Starting with the why of your blog is going to help you lay down the strongest foundation.

Why?

Well, blogging is hard. There are going to be moments you want to just give up and give in. *All* bloggers have been there (including me). But being able to go back to my why, my true purpose of starting a blog, helps me navigate the difficult moments. The moments I just want to walk away and never look back.

Your why is going to be crucial to the success of your blog. It's going to keep you moving forward. It's going to remind you of the reason behind your blog. It's going to motivate you.

But you have to dig deep. You have to explore the *real* and *raw* reasons why you are starting your blog. It's about more than making an income. It's about more than sharing your stories. It's about creating community. It's about healing through the power of words. It's about giving yourself a voice.

My why…

I want to show women that it's safe to share their past. I want women to know that there is power in their past and it does not have a hold over them. I want to be able to show my children that because of my past, I was able to create a business that changed the world. I want women to see, feel, and know they are worthy of everything they want to achieve and everything they want to be. I want women to accept themselves as whole and build businesses using their stories and their magic.

I now want you to grab a piece of paper and just write. Don't overthink it. Just begin to write whatever comes to mind when you think about why you want to start a blog. You can go back and refine it once you're done, but just begin. Be in the moment and write down everything that comes to you.

The best part of this is that there is no right or wrong. This is so incredibly personal to you. You don't even need to tell anyone your why. This is for you. If you're struggling with this, I also heard a great thing on a podcast once about creating your why.

There are a couple of different whys that you can write. Your totally and completely selfish why. Maybe you want to travel or have another baby or whatever *you* truly want. The second is the deeper and more personal why. The real and raw reason you are doing what you are doing. The why that is deeply ingrained inside of you. This is the why that keeps you awake, keeps you moving toward your dreams even on the days when you just want to walk away.

Once you have your first draft done of your why, go back and read it. Does it feel like it sums up all of the reasons that you want to start a blog? Refine it, rewrite it and then post it somewhere that you will be able to see it every single day. Keep it close to you so that you have this reminder.

Your why is going to be crucial to the success of your blog. It's going to keep you moving forward.

Chapter 3

Before words ever hit your website

Laying the foundation means that you need to lay down the groundwork before you even begin to think about writing on your blog. Blogging is a multifaceted being. There are so many moving parts that you need to ensure that you lay down a strong foundation before you can just begin to blog.

I didn't do that. I just started blogging because I thought of it as a hobby. You picked up this book because you are serious about wanting to blog, which means it isn't just a hobby for you. Blogging will open up many different avenues for you to take when it comes to creating your own business. I love the fact that blogging gives you the opportunity to create YOUR business YOUR way. You can create your business in any way you can imagine.

Before you can even begin to move forward with blogging, you need to figure out and decide how much time you can dedicate to it. Blogging is a full-time job. You need to ensure that you can dedicate enough time to reach the success that you imagine.

I want to take a moment here and say something…

You will see on Pinterest, and other places, things like this…

How I Made $5,000 From My Blog in 30 Days
How I Made $30,000 From My Blog

I want to get super clear here. I am in no way saying that this is impossible, BUT I am saying this isn't the norm. Blogging is a long-term strategy. You need to be in it for the long haul because it takes time to build a community, build trust, and show your audience that you are an expert in your niche. Be patient. You can reach these goals but they will take time.

The last thing I want to add is that when you see these pins on Pinterest, these bloggers who are saying this are discounting all of the hard work that they put in prior to those 30 days. Just remember that they already had a strong foundation down before making that money.

Now back to laying your foundation.

Grab your planner and begin to see how much time you can commit to blogging. As a beginner, writing a blog post can take you anywhere from 3-5 hours. That is only the writing portion. That doesn't include everything that comes after the writing phase.

I would recommend starting with 1 blog post per week or if even that is too much, start with 2 blog posts a month. You can always increase as you go and get more efficient with writing your blogs.

The important part to remember when it comes to this step is to be completely honest with yourself. You want your blog to work around your life, not the other way around. I recently changed from writing 3 blog posts per week to sticking with 2 blog posts per week. I did this because my life got busy and I want to ensure that my blog is still fitting in the lifestyle that I want to lead.

Now that you have an idea of how much time you can commit to having a blog, it's time to grab some paper and start setting some goals for yourself. You may be wondering how to set goals for something that you have never done before but I will give you some examples of how you can do that.

As bloggers, we tend to get caught up in our numbers. It's a numbers game—and it's great to have goals set when it comes to numbers—but there are also other goals you can begin to create. What do I mean by it being a numbers game? We want our readers to keep growing so we are constantly looking to see how many visitors we are getting to our site. We want our bounce rate to be low because that means that we are keeping our readers on our site.

We tend to value the number of followers we have when it comes to social media, and blogging is no different. BUT I want you to remember that you can have five readers per month and that is perfectly fine. Throw away the concept of numbers before it consumes your life. I recommend keeping track of them once a month, but not focusing on them. No matter if you have 50 readers or 500 readers, you are making a difference to someone.

I always start my clients by setting goals of 30 days, 3 months, 6 months, and 12-months. You'll be able to reevaluate your goals after 30 days (and at any time) so this is just to get started somewhere.

To help you get started with these goals, in the next chapter, I'm going to break down the nine different pieces that you'll need to create these goals and your vision for blogging.

No matter if you have 50 readers or 500 readers, you are making a difference to someone.

Chapter 4

The "Nine Areas of Your Blogging Vision"

I absolutely love teaching this to everyone and anyone who is willing to listen. Creating goals when you're a beginner blogger can feel intimidating and not really worth doing since you haven't started. But by taking these areas--and using them to create your vision and your goals--you will have a better game plan for success.

You're going to want to grab a giant piece of paper and break it up into nine sections. You can write in the sections themselves or you can use Post-It notes to add to the squares. Let's cover the nine topics now.

Education. Now, this area is so important. I believe that to truly be successful, you'll always need to learn new things. I am a lifelong learner and I think everyone should be. When you focus on this piece of the puzzle, you don't only have to focus on your niche.

This can cover anything and everything that you want to learn. What are the classes or courses that you want to take? Write them all into this box.

Social. Social is all about connecting with other bloggers. Write down where and how you can connect with other bloggers that are both in and out of your niche. A few areas where you can connect with other bloggers are Facebook groups, Instagram and LinkedIn.

Monetization. This is one of the fun pieces of your vision. I want you to start brainstorming all of the ways that you can and want to make money. Think outside the box. Yes, you can do ads on your blog but think of other ways. Personally, I'm not a fan of ads on blogs, so I try to teach my clients to make money their way.

A few ways that clients of mine have made money through their blogs.

1. Journals. She sells physical and digital copies of her different types of journals. She sells these through her website and through Etsy.
2. Coaching clients. Coaching is a HUGE industry and it is a great way to help your ideal reader. You can offer 1:1 coaching or group coaching within your niche and expertise.

3. Books they wrote. Hint, hint. This book is a way that I can make money through my blog. You can write nonfiction or fiction books.
4. Services they provided. A few examples of services that you can provide are virtual assistant, beauty services, freelance services and so much more.
5. Digital printables. Like the journals above, you can create so many different digital printables. A few examples are recipes, planners, eBooks, calendars, workbooks and more.

The ideas are endless and you can create them to fit your expertise and your knowledge.

Outreach. I never thought about this category when I first started blogging. I wish I had focused more on it. Outreach is about showcasing your expertise in front of other audiences. This is where you can begin to write guest blog posts, share infographics that you have created, be a speaker on a podcast and so many more options.

You want to start your outreach as soon as you begin blogging. A good way to begin this outreach is to head to Google and type in your niche + guest blogging. You can also head to your social media (for example, IG) and look through your followers. More than likely, you are already following others who are in your niche and shoulder niches. These are great people to reach out to. This will help to improve your DA (domain authority) as well as reach already established audiences.

Growth. As I stated above, blogging is a numbers game that we can get caught up in so, of course, it has to be part of your vision and goals. It will fit into this category. When you're first beginning, you really won't know what numbers are realistic, and that's totally fine. Write down a number for 30 days and then reevaluate at that time to see if you need to change the numbers you wrote for the next 3 months.

Schedule. We talked about this in the last chapter. Knowing how much time you have to write is important. Knowing how much time you have to do the other pieces of blogging is important. This will change over time. Start small and build up from there. Remember, blogging is about more than just writing and publishing your blog posts. Blogging is also compromised of social media outreach, sharing your blog post in multiple locations and researching.

Foundational. You can begin to brainstorm everything you need to run your blog smoothly. This category covers everything from your website to social media to email platforms. What do you need to be successful when it comes to blogging?

Desire. Focus on what it is that YOU want. This will tie into what you wrote down as your why. As the Netflix character, Lucifer says, "What is it that you truly desire?"

Mindset. This is one of the most important categories you can focus on. What do you need to do or want to learn when it comes to your mindset? I struggled with my mindset for a long time. There are still days when I do. Mindset is all about the attitudes that you have established. Your mindset is going to be influenced by those in your circle, your childhood and the words that you repeat in your head. These can be negative and positive.

Write all of your ideas into this category so that you can begin to reach them. A few ways to help you begin to improve your mindset are affirmations, meditation, and journaling.

These are the nine categories that you should focus on when it comes to creating your blogging vision and goals. Have fun and take your time. You are in no rush when it comes to creating your blog. This is all going to help you create that strong foundation that you need to have in place before you begin blogging.

9 areas of your

blogging vision

BLOGGINGYOURSTORY.COM

Education	Social	Monetization
Outreach	Growth	Schedule
Foundational	Desire	Mindset

By taking these areas--and using them to create your vision and your goals--you will have a better game plan for success.

Chapter 5

Choosing your blogging niche

It's time for you to decide what it is you want to write about. Having a niche is incredibly important when it comes to blogging. A few of the benefits of choosing a blogging niche are…

1. Better SEO ranking
2. A defined target audience
3. Speaking directly to that target audience in their language
4. You showcase your expertise
5. You can build your credibility

I have created 5 lists that will help you to narrow down your focus when it comes to choosing your blogging niche. These lists are going to help you organize your thoughts and get you on track to picking the niche that is right for you.

List #1: Write down everything you are passionate about. When I started blogging, I was in the mental health/self-care/self-love niche. Part of what I do still covers those pieces.

This list will help you do a giant brain dump on what it is that you love to do. Write everything down because the next four lists are going to help you narrow it down even more. This is only the beginning.

I don't want you to overthink this list. It's meant to be everything and anything that you are passionate about. Just write this list out.

1. Cooking
2. Cleaning
3. Scrapbooking
4. Hiking
5. Reading
6. Journaling
7. Helping people through their problems

List #2: What topics from list one do you know the best? We all have passions. Some of those passions we have, we aren't skilled at. That's okay. A passion is there for us to explore. When it comes to blogging, you want to make sure you have passion and expertise. This list will help you narrow down what it is that you are an expert in.

With list two, I want you to try and narrow it down to the top five. Remember these are the topics you know the most about. If you have less than five, that's okay. It means you have even less narrowing down to do than those people who have five.

List #3: Take your top five and break them into categories. On the top of a piece of paper, I need you to draw five umbrellas. Well, just the top shape of an umbrella. In each umbrella, take one of your top fives and write it in. Those five things will be your main topics for now.

Under each of those umbrellas and main topics, I want you to write about what it is that you can talk about. Write everything down you can think of that has anything to do with the main topic. Remember, you're still in brainstorming mode, and the more information you can write down, the better off you'll know and understand the niche you decide to choose.

Looking through these, you'll begin to realize that you know more about certain topics than other topics. These are the niche ideas that you are going to carry into list four.

List #4: Write down what you can teach under those topics. By this list, I'm hoping that you're down to two or three main topics that you want to talk about. With the remaining topics you've chosen, I want you to brainstorm all the things you can teach.

As we look back on these topics, you will realize that you have learned things throughout all of your experiences. These are the pieces that you can teach about. We don't look at our experiences as being teaching moments but that is exactly what they are. More than likely you won't realize what you are learning while you are living through the experience but when you look back, you will see what is it that you have learned. Line these experiences up with the topics you are choosing.

This is a little bit different from the above list because maybe not everything that you know, you can teach. However, what you wrote on list three means that you can learn all of those things and someday begin to teach them.

The best thing to do with this list is to get super specific when it comes to what you can teach. Break it down into each step like I explained above.

List #5: All about the research. List five is where you're going to begin to do some keyword research to see what topics are most searched when it comes to that niche. I'm hoping by this point, you've narrowed down your big list from step one to only one or two niche ideas.

This step is going to be time-consuming. You're going to want to keep track of the SD (SEO Difficulty) when it comes to the keywords that you are typing in. Also, remember that you can use short tail (1-2 words) and long-tail keywords (a phrase) when looking up keywords.

5 lists to create to

NARROW DOWN YOUR BLOGGING NICHE

01 Write down everything you are passionate about.

02 What topics from list one do you know the best?

03 Take your top five and break them into categories.

04 Write down what you can teach under those topics.

05 All about your research for your keywords.

When you create these lists, you're going to want a mixture of keywords with different SDs. The websites that I love to use to research these keywords are Ubersuggest, Moz, Keyword Chef and Google Keyword Planner just to name a few. You want some easy (under 50), some moderate (50-70) and then you want some that are difficult (70-100). The higher the number, the harder it will be to rank for that keyword because there is more competition. There are many different factors that are used to determine the ranking of a keyword.

Now that we have you closer to choosing your blogging niche, it's time to talk about your blogging audience. This step may even help you finally decide on your blogging niche.

> *Having a niche means you are speaking to the people that you want to speak to*
>
> *—Samantha*

Chapter 6

Getting to know your blogging audience

To be successful as a blogger, we need to know our audience. We need to know who we want on our website and why. Without knowing this, we can't write. We're left stumbling around in the dark and wondering why no one is reading our blog.

We need to know their pain points and their struggles.
We need to know what they are searching for on search engines. Think about the words you are typing into Google.
We need to know the kind of language that they understand most. Think about the type of words that you are typing into Google.
We need to know the reason they come to our blog and not someone else's.
We need to know them inside out.

Before we get too deep, let's start with how we can define our ideal reader and audience. You want to figure out who you're writing for. Who do you want to read your blog? Narrowing this down helps you figure out what topics to write about, which blog categories to have, and what type of content your ideal readers are searching for.

Defining your ideal reader can feel daunting at first. Especially if your blog is a lifestyle blog. You may have multiple different ideal readers but there is still a way for you to define who they are and how you can reach them.

You want readers to come to your blog. But not only readers. You want relevant readers to be attracted to your blog. Just getting people to your website doesn't mean they're meant to be there. This is why defining your ideal reader is so important. It really isn't about numbers. It's about bringing the readers that you know need your information to your site. This doesn't mean that you won't have readers that come to your blog only to find out what you offer isn't what they were looking for. It means that you are consistently trying to focus on what a certain group of people are looking for.

Here are five questions you should ask yourself to help you define your ideal audience.

1| What niche are you writing in? This is such a big first step. You need to narrow down your niche so that you know what you are writing about. Ideas for niches are lifestyle, blogging, food, personal finance, fashion, and so many more. Being clear on WHAT you are writing about will help you narrow down WHO you are writing for. The lists from the previous chapter are going to help you narrow this down.

There are niches that have more competition than others, but don't let that stop you. If it's something you are truly passionate about, then you can make it happen. Don't let a competitive niche stop you from starting your blog. There is always room for you in ANY niche that you choose. Just be yourself. There are people out there looking for you.

2| What problems are you solving? Now that you have a niche picked out (or at least narrowed down), what problem can you solve for your ideal reader? What are their pain points? What do they struggle with on a daily basis? What keeps them up at night? What are they Googling?

Being able to answer these questions will help you to narrow down your readers again. Were you in their shoes at one point? Maybe your ideal reader is YOU, a few years ago. Make a list of all of these questions to help you know what you are going to blog about.

3| What are the benefits that your ideal reader will get from reading your blog posts? Now that you have them on your site, what are they going to get out of it? Remember that you are the one doing the writing, but that doesn't mean the writing is for you. You are writing your blog to help your ideal client.

They are on your site for a reason. What is that reason? List all of the benefits they will gain from being there. What are they learning? How do they feel when they're on your site?

4| What products or services are you going to be selling to them? If you have or are wanting to start a business to go along with your blog, you are going to want to know what your offers will be. This will help you to narrow down your ideal reader.

If you already have a business, you know who your ideal client is. Your ideal reader will be the same. You want to connect with them and that is the purpose of your blog. You want to teach them about what you do and why you do it.

If you don't have a business yet, think about what you want to offer. This will help determine your ideal reader. You want your ideal reader and your ideal client to be the same. This allows you to grow your blog as well as your business.

5| Write down the qualities of your reader. This is the fun part. Think of it as creating your blogging avatar. What do they look like? What do they do for fun? Do they own a business? Do they have children? Get personal and think about what it is that your ideal reader is doing.

This really allows you to be in their shoes. Gives you a glimpse into their life. For example, when I first started blogging, my ideal reader was who I was at that time. It was a woman who was sexually assaulted but hadn't dealt with it yet. She was struggling with self-love and putting her needs before others. She was a mother who felt like every day was a struggle to stay afloat.

Get personal and think about what it is that your ideal reader is doing.

Defining Your Ideal Blogging Audience

- *What niche are you blogging in?*
- *What problems are you solving?*
- *What are the benefits you want your readers to get?*
- *What products/services are you going to sell?*
- *Write down the qualities of your readers.*

Over the years, my ideal reader has changed, and that's okay. It means that my brand is evolving and who I'm writing for is changing. Start where you are now and who you want to be reading your blog at this moment.

Make coming up with your ideal reader fun. Draw the person out if you're an artist. Write their qualities down if you're not an artist. This is a great place to start your blogging journey. It allows you to get super clear on your intentions for blogging and who you want to read everything that you write.

You now have ways to help you define your ideal audience, but let's learn how to understand them on an even deeper level.

Most of the time, we are our ideal reader. By that I mean, we were once in their shoes. We once held the same beliefs, the same struggles, the same thoughts as they do now. We are writing about what we have learned to move us past those points in our life.

We understand them because we *were* them. Allowing ourselves to understand our readers means that we can connect with them on a deeper level. It means that we can speak their language. This process doesn't end but it does continually evolve.

There are deeper ways for us to understand our readers and, as a blogger, that's what we want. We're blogging as a way to connect with people. We're blogging to share our stories and our passions. Learning how to understand your audience on a deeper level begins now.

Engage with your readers. This will allow you to open up communication with those who are reading your blog. It also means that you give them permission to ask questions and to know that they will be answered. If you aren't clear on something that a reader says or asks, ask them to clarify it. This will show them that you truly want to have a discussion.

Listen to your readers. Most of the time, listening is more important than your writing. Listen to their concerns. Listen to their questions. Listen to the comments that they're leaving you. Listen without the intent to reply right away. We think that writing is the most important blogging skill, but it truly is listening to your readers. What is it that they want?

What is it that they are craving? What is it that they are searching for?

Listen to how your writing sounds. I seem to say a similar phrase to my kids often. “It isn’t what you said, but how you said it.” The same goes for your blog writing. You want to make your blog posts conversational. You don’t want to make it sound like you’re talking down to your readers. You want to invite discussion and invoke thinking. You want to engage with your readers on a human level.

We’ve all had moments when someone sent us a message through text or email and you have no context with how to take it. Avoid this when writing your blog post. This doesn’t mean that you can’t be controversial. It means to do so with respect to your readers.

Share your vulnerability. This will help your reader know where you are coming from and why you are blogging about what you are blogging about. If your ideal reader is who you used to be, this means that you are connecting to them through this shared vulnerability. When they are currently feeling what you used to feel, writing in an emotion that they understand will bring you closer to your reader. Vulnerability connects people. We all want to know we are not alone in any of our journeys.

Fear takes over and has a way of talking us out of sharing our stories. Once we look fear in the face, nothing can stop us.

Be interested in what they have to say. This comes back to the tip above, listen to your readers, but takes it a step further. Be interested in what they're telling you. Don't just respond to comments to respond. Take the time and effort to give a thoughtful response to their question, concern or comment. Show them that you appreciate them taking the time to comment when life is busy. Truly thank them for showing up. Without them, you wouldn't have readers.

Blogging is about your audience. At the end of the day, that truly is what blogging is about. You can write for yourself, but you need to do that with your readers in mind. Without readers, you are just taking up space on the internet. You have amazing things to share. You have stories that need to be heard.

We get caught up in pageviews and followers. I know because there are days that I do. Those are the days that I begin to question myself. Those are the days that I allow my head to take over, and I forget about those that are showing up every day on my website.

Once I remember to bring my audience into my blog, my journey and thoughts change. I strive to do better and be better for them. I take the time to thank them. I take the time to learn about who they are.

To stand out in the crowd of bloggers, you must love your audience. You must learn to engage with your audience. You must learn to listen to your audience. Understanding your blogging audience is the best way to gain true readership and, as a blogger, that's what we want.

We want dedicated readers that will come back to our website every day. In order for that to happen, you need to be dedicated to them.

To stand out in a crowd of bloggers, you must love your audience.

Chapter 7

Choosing your "blogging pillars"

You may be wondering why I introduced the blogging audience before choosing your blogging pillars. It's because knowing your blogging audience is also going to help you choose and narrow down your niche. They are interconnected and go hand in hand.

I love to really simplify the blogging process. There are so many moving parts that it can quickly become overwhelming. In this chapter, we are going to make sure that your site is set up to benefit your readers and ensure that you are getting your message across to those ideal readers in a way that they understand.

Your blogging pillars are going to consist of the main topics and ideas that your blog covers. I am not talking about blogging categories here even though you can use your blogging pillars as a few of your blogging categories.

All of the content I create is created with these blogging pillars in mind. They are the biggest pieces of my business. They are what I want to teach my clients and readers about when they come to my website. It is a way to break down your niche into the pieces that are most important to you. This IS the foundation of your blog.

My blogging pillars are the same as my business pillars because they cover all the aspects of my business and blog. My blogging pillars are...

1. Storytelling
2. Healing and Transformation
3. Acceptance and Self-Love
4. Blogging
5. Motivation and Organization

When it comes to creating your blogging pillars, there's no right or wrong way to do so. If you look above at mine, you will notice that some have two words. That's because, to me, those two words go hand in hand, and I couldn't have one without the other.

You may be wondering where to actually begin when it comes to creating these pillars for your blog. I want you to think about your niche. Write your niche down on a piece of paper.

We have done this exercise before as well in choosing a niche, but I want you to write down what it is that you can teach in the niche.

These questions are going to help you start to narrow down the content that you already create. The content pillars are for you to know. They are going to help you to create blog content, social media content, digital products and more. These blogging pillars are going to be an integral part of your blog, so this isn't a step that you want to skip.

What are you currently talking about when it comes to your niche?

What do you find that you are super passionate about when it comes to your niche?

What content do you currently have that has the most views or most comments?

Are there specific questions about your niche that you love to answer?

What are your strengths when it comes to your specific blogging niche?

Think of these pillars as the foundation of your blog. They are there to show you what it is within your niche that you talk about. These pillars are showcasing your expertise inside of your blogging niche.

All of the content I create is created with these blogging pillars in mind. They are the biggest pieces of my business.. This IS the foundation of your blog.

Chapter 8

Picking your blogging platform

I often hear new bloggers (or women who want to start a blog) ask what host they should use. There are so many out there that this is probably the most overwhelming process to begin your blog. I would even say that it's probably one of the reasons that most people keep putting off their blog.

And the thing is, everyone is going to have an opinion. My opinion will differ from thousands of other bloggers' opinions, and that is okay.   Every time someone goes into a Facebook group and asks this question, the answers are varied.

I love Wix. I'll tell everyone that, but I seem to have a different opinion from others. So, while I recommend Wix any chance I get, I also remind them that everyone has an opinion and it really comes down to what you are needing and looking for in a website platform.

In order to figure out what the best blogging platform is, you must first figure out what your blogging goals are. I always recommend starting with goals. It will give you a bigger picture of what you truly want to happen with your blog.

When it comes to choosing your blogging platform, knowing where you want your blog to go is incredibly important. In order to decide what is important, what you love, and what you need, answering these questions is going to help you narrow it all down.

Which platforms have you already checked out? Make a list of the platforms that you've already started to research and ones that you still want to look at.

Are you looking for a drag and drop website, or do you want to create your own? Wix is a platform that offers drag and drop websites. If you aren't really strong when it comes to technology, it's a great option to have.

What is your budget for the website host? There will be some website platforms that offer monthly payments and some website platforms that offer only yearly options. Make sure you get clear on what you can afford.

Do you need to purchase a website URL? I ALWAYS recommend purchasing your own domain. Normally the platform you choose will give you an option to purchase your domain. Namecheap.com is also a great choice to find your domain. This is one of the first ways that you can brand your blog.

Do you need the option of an eCommerce website? This is an important question to answer because you need to ensure that the platform you chose has the option of adding a way to monetize when you are ready. You don't want to choose and set up a platform ONLY to realize that you can't monetize the way that you thought.

Does it come with an SSL certificate? You should always have an SSL certificate. It gives your readers and customers added protection to know that their information is safe. An SSL certificate lets your readers know that it authenticates your website and enables an encrypted connection.

What do they offer for website support? I will say this, it's the one thing I don't really like when it comes to Wix. Their customer support is hard to get a hold of and it can take some time. Usually, I can manage without them and if I can't, when I call, they call me back within five minutes. Knowing how you can contact them for support is important.

Does it allow you to have website contributors? Having an option to have website contributors may help you in the future. You can add additional blog writers to your website if you want. This wasn't important to me when I was setting up, but it's a great idea to look into if you want to create a forum or have guest bloggers be able to write on your website without being the middle man.

Are you going to go with a paid or free site? I ALWAYS, ALWAYS, ALWAYS suggest that you go with a paid site. BUT I do understand that sometimes it isn't possible. I started on a free platform when I began blogging in 2014 to see if I liked it. If you choose the free route, you won't be able to connect to your own domain.

List aspects of your favourite sites. What did you love about them? What features did you hate and want to avoid? Start looking up different websites and keeping track of what you loved about them and what you hated. This is a great way to get clear on what it is that is important to you. Now go have fun deciding what is important to you when it comes to your blogging platform.

Get clear on what is important to you in a website. Everyone will have an opinion but it truly does not matter.

Chapter 9

Branding your blog

Branding seems to be one of the most important parts of any business these days. You want to ensure that your clients and readers know who you are, and branding plays a HUGE part in that.

I never worried about branding when I first started. I just wrote my blog posts and crossed my fingers that someone, anyone, would read it. That was the objective back then. Well, that's still the objective, but now I have a better plan in place.

Branding is about more than just what your company looks like. It's about how it makes your clients and readers feel. It's about what you talk about and who you are as a person. Branding encompasses the whole person, not just the business.

I really want to share with you a checklist to use to keep you on track as you go through the process of creating your blogging brand.

One: Describe your ideal reader. Every coach that you will talk with will tell you that this is the first step. Get specific. I actually found through the use of insights on my Facebook business page, who my ideal client really was. It helped me narrow it down. I recommend setting up a Facebook business page because it allows you to see who is viewing your page (location, sex of people, and times they are on your page). This helps you see who is interested in the topics that you're blogging about.

Two: What are your blog goals? Knowing and being clear on your blogging goals will help you to communicate, connect, and empower your readers in a way that only you can.

Three: Your blog name. Are you going to have a specific blog name? What will that be? You want it to showcase what it is that you do while still being creative.

Four: Colours and Hex codes. What colours do you want on your website and logo? What colours represent your ideal client? Look into the psychology of colour as well. Make sure that you choose between 3-6 colours. This will give you colours that you use often as well as complimentary colours that you can use every once in a while.

Five: Your expertise. Have you narrowed down what you're teaching your readers? This will make a difference in how you brand yourself.

Six: What products/services are you going to have available? This is a big part of your branding. What are you offering your readers? Even if you currently aren't offering products or services, brainstorm ideas for what you want to have.

Seven: Your story. What are you willing to share with your audience to help you connect with them? Remember that your branding is about more than just your business. It is about what you bring to your business and who you are as a person.

Eight: Your unique perspective. There are no new niches out there. There are just different perspectives on the ones that already exist. How are you unique from those that are in the same niche as you? Think of ways you can teach your readers outside of what your competitors are doing (I really hate the word competitors).

Nine: What is your mission statement? Have fun with this. Mission statements don't have to be all serious. This is a perfect place to connect to your readers and let them know why you have your blog.

My mission statement is…

Giving women a voice after being silenced.

Ten: How do you want your reader to feel when they are on your site? This is important. Do you want them to feel calm and relaxed? Do you want them to feel pumped up and inspired? Get clear on how you want them to feel.

Eleven: How can you best communicate these feelings? What are the ways you can get your clients to feel on your site? What words can you use to ignite these emotions? These words are all going to come from you. If you need some inspiration, look up on Pinterest, words of the year.

Twelve: Your content calendar. How often are you going to be sharing blog posts with your ideal reader? Create your content calendar around your schedule. You can always add more blog posts once you get the hang of it. I always recommend that you start small with either once a week or every other week.

There is no right amount of blog posts that you can publish. This comes down to how much time you can commit to blogging. I want you to remember that quality is better than quantity.

Thirteen: Pages on your website. Besides your blog, what are the pages you want to have on your website? The pages that you should start with on your blog are: About me, Blog, Contact Me, and

Legal pages (disclaimer, terms & conditions, and privacy policy).

Fourteen: Blogging toolkit. What tools do you need to ensure that you can help your clients in the way that you want? Your blogging toolkit will contain everything that you use to ensure that your blog is running smoothly. The resources that I have in my toolkit are Canva, Flodesk, Wix, and Later.

Fifteen: Set up your social media. You want to try and get your blog name as your social media handles if you can. This will ensure that you have a consistent brand. Your readers will know who to look up on any of your social media platforms.

Sixteen: Implement your plan. Now, it's time to get started. You have prepared yourself, so in order to get your readers to your website, you need to start showing it.

As you can see, branding your blog is about more than just the colours on your website.
It encompasses all aspects of yourself as well as your blog.

Branding is about more than just what your company looks like. It's about how it makes your clients and readers feel.

Brand Your Blog Checklist

- ☐ Describe your ideal reader
- ☐ What are your blog goals
- ☐ Your blog name
- ☐ Colours and Hex codes
- ☐ Your expertise
- ☐ Products/services you will have
- ☐ Your story
- ☐ Your blogging toolkit
- ☐ Pages on your website
- ☐ Your unique perspective
- ☐ What is your mission statement
- ☐ How do you want your readers to feel
- ☐ How can you communicate those feelings?
- ☐ Your content calendar
- ☐ Set up your social media
- ☐ Implement your plan

Chapter 10

Blogging habits to add to your life

There are certain blogging habits you can add to your daily life to begin to uplevel when it comes to your blog. You started a blog with hopes that it would create an impact. Now is the time to start making that impact that you were hoping for.

I am not an expert in knowing what the benefits of habits are. Habits are the things in your life that you want to be consistent with. Consistency is key to moving forward in ANYTHING that you do, so it makes sense that creating habits that are going to move you forward will be of benefit.

Here are the benefits I've seen in my personal life when it comes to habits.

1| Habits give me a daily focus. As a creative entrepreneur, I will admit that my head can sometimes be all over the place. Having my daily habits written out gives me a clear focus on what I NEED and WANT to do every day. I have certain things that I do immediately when waking up. They include doing a guided meditation and writing out affirmations. Those two things get me focused for my day and ready to get work done.

2| My healing journey is going deeper. With the habits that I've written down to do daily, I've realized that I can go deeper on my healing journey. I'm beginning to learn more about myself, and that affects every part of my life, including my blogging.

3| My days run smoother. Because I'm gaining focus throughout my day, it is naturally running smoother. I can create a to-do list and have the energy to do it because I have time for what is making my life happy. Plus, my kids are noticing a difference in how I talk to them.

It's time to cover the blogging habits to add to your life to begin improving your blog. Knowing how often you want to schedule new content is going to help with some of these blogging habits.

1| Write every day. You don't need to finish a blog post every day, but it's a good idea to get some writing in every single day. It will help you keep up with blogging, but it will also get you in the habit of writing.

2| Create a blog schedule that you can stick to. I always say to start small. This allows you to grow as you go. You can also do less as you go along. That's what I'm doing because my schedule is changing due to clients changing. This schedule is all about what works for you. By creating a schedule, you are creating a habit of publishing new content.

3| Post to your social media every day. This is important so that you can continue to be consistent and that your followers see you every day. You can break up your blog post into multiple, different social media posts and reuse them on each platform that you have. This way you're showing up, but you don't have to keep creating NEW social media content. REUSE, REUSE, REUSE! It will save your sanity.

4| Comment on other blog posts by bloggers in your niche. You want to get your name out there, so start commenting. Stop hiding behind your blog, and put yourself out there. Commenting is a great way to get the visibility you may not otherwise have gotten.

5| Share your blog post to multiple locations. Do this every day. Remember, the real work of a blogger starts AFTER they hit publish. Create a Trello board that keeps track of all the FB groups you're in and on what days you can share your blog post. Share to Mix, Twitter, your personal FB, IG, LinkedIn. SHARE, SHARE, SHARE.

6| Practice creating graphics. Graphics can really grab the attention of your followers and readers. Practice every day by creating graphics to use on your social media and in your blog post. Canva is one of the best tools to help you create graphics. They have templates that you can use and change up to match your branding.

Essential Blogging Habits

- Write every day
- Create a blog schedule you can stick with
- Post to your social media every day
- Comment on blogs in your niche
- Share your blog post to multiple locations
- Practice creating graphics

bloggingyourstory.com

I use them multiple times a day for every graphic that I create for my blog and business.

I am all about creating a plan to help you move forward. I'm a very organized person and it helps to keep me on track. So here are some tips to help you create a plan that's going to work for you.

By creating a plan to work on these blogging habits every day, you will NOT overwhelm yourself when you begin to implement these habits.

1| Grab a daily calendar or a blank piece of paper. Start with 2 pieces of paper so you can first brainstorm EVERYTHING you need to get done for the day. I create separate lists for home and for my blog and business. Your everything list will be written down on one of those blank pieces of paper.

2| I recommend time blocking. I would start with 2-3 hour time blocks because then you have a longer period of time to get things finished. It is easier than just doing one-hour increments. This will be easiest for you to do when you have designated work hours during the day. Your second piece of paper will be for you to write down your time blocking hours.

3| Grab your EVERYTHING list and your time blocking piece of paper and start to transfer what you need to do onto your time blocking page. Do the most important things first and then work your way down. You are now organized to be more productive during the day, as well as adding in the blogging habits that are going to begin to change your blogging game.

You now have a time plan to add all of these habits into your day. You will realize that some of these blogging habits you already do on a daily basis, and you already have them written down on your everything list. Just add in the ones that you don't have to your everything list onto your time blocking if you have space.

That is how you begin to add blogging habits into your daily life. Easy as pie.

Final word

Now is your time

I wanted to take a moment to again say thank you for buying this book. Creating a strong foundation for your blog is the best way to see success. There are so many moving pieces when it comes to blogging that it can feel overwhelming before you even begin.

By creating a plan and having a book like this, you can begin the process slowly. You can ensure that you have a solid foundation that will help you move forward and fall in love with the blogging process.

> *Let your words make a difference in someone's life.*
>
> *—Samantha*

Your blogging glossary

I covered a lot of terminology in this book and I know that it can get overwhelming fast. I wanted to share with you some of the blogging terms that you will need to learn. You'll see these terms used often when it comes to talking about blogging. Some of these words are not in this book but they are still good to know because you will come across them as you begin to blog.

AFFILIATE LINK: This is a link where you can purchase a product and the blogger will receive money for sending you there. For example, I have an affiliate link for an AMAZING Pinterest course that I have taken. That means that when you purchase this course, I will receive compensation for your purchase. What I recommend when it comes to getting affiliate links is to make sure that you are promoting products/services that you use and that your blog readers are going to find helpful. Reach out to brands and small businesses that you love to see if they offer an affiliate program option.

ALTERNATE TEXT: This means a word or a phrase that describes your photo and graphic that you place in your blog post. Graphics cannot be read by the algorithms on search engines. Alternate text is there to tell the search engines what your photo is of and is about. It also helps those who are visually impaired to be able to access and know what your graphics are about.

ANCHOR TEXT: This is the word or set of words that you highlight in your blog post and link to another website or another blog post. This refers to the text itself. For example, last week I spoke about how I became to be a blogging coach. See how those words are blue? They are my anchor text and will take you to a blog post that I have previously published.

BACKLINK: This is any link that is on your blog that sends your reader to another page.

BOUNCE RATE: This describes the % of people who look at your blog and then leave. The lower your bounce rate, the better. It means that your readers are staying on your blog longer.

CATEGORY: This is how you organize your blog posts. When someone goes to your blog page on your website, you want them to know what it is that you talk about. I want you to think of these categories as the navigation bar of your blogging page. The categories will be posted at the top of your blogging page for your readers to easily see.

COMMENTS: Comments can be found at the bottom of your blog posts. Your readers can leave them for you. You should always reply to the comments of your readers. This is a great place to find what your clients are struggling with and get new ideas for blog posts.

CTA or CALL TO ACTION: At the end of every blog post, you should give your reader a CTA. This means that you are giving them an action to complete. Whether that is to comment on a blog post, to follow you on a specific social media platform, or to sign up for your email list. There are so many options for you to create your CTAs. Just make sure that they are relevant to your reader.

CONTENT CALENDAR: This is your plan for the content you are going to publish on your website. It can include the content that you will also publish on your social media.

DOMAIN AUTHORITY: This is a scale from 1-100. The higher your domain authority is, the higher you will rank in search engine searches. Domain Authority is based on data and uses dozens of factors in its calculations. *Domain Authority is calculated by evaluating multiple factors, including linking root domains and a total number of links, into a single DA score. This score can then be used when comparing websites or tracking the "ranking strength" of a website over time. (Source: Moz)*

EVERGREEN CONTENT: This is content that is always relevant. It isn't seasonal. You can reuse your evergreen content throughout the year and continue to bring in new readers to your blog.

FAVICON: This is the little graphic that will appear when you type in your blog URL into your browser. I have mine set as my logo. On Wix, there is an area during the setup of your website where you will be able to upload an image for the favicon.

GUEST BLOG POST: This is where you write a blog post on someone else's blog. This is a great way to reach a new audience. Make sure that when you choose a blog to write on, that it is somewhere that your ideal reader is going to also be reading.

HEADER: This is the part of your website pages that lets your readers know what page they are on. It can include your logo or tagline as well.

HEX CODES: Hex codes are the hexadecimal way of identifying colours. If you're looking to find hex codes for colours you love, I recommend using imagecolorpicker.com On this website, you'll be able to upload photos that have colours you love, click on the colour and the HEX code will be shown.

HYPERLINK: This is the clickable content that the anchor text sends you to. It is referring to the link and not to the text itself. Using a hyperlink allows your readers to more easily navigate your site and gives them additional resources to use.

KEYWORDS: This can refer to short-tail keywords or long-tail keywords. These are the topics that are most relevant to your ideal reader. The keywords that you pick will help to showcase your expertise in the niche that you choose. You want these keywords to be words that your ideal reader will be using to search for what you talk about.

LEAD MAGNET: This is a freebie that you offer to your readers. A lead magnet is a great way to get your ideal readers to sign up for your email list. I use Canva to create my lead magnets and I use Flodesk to deliver them to those who sign up for them.

LONG-TAIL KEYWORD: These are super-specific keywords that your ideal reader is going to be searching for on search engines. They are searched less often than short-tail keywords and are usually longer in length.

META DESCRIPTION: This is the part of your website that describes what a particular page is about. You want to include a keyword in this description so that it will help your SEO and will help the search engines know what your page is about.

NICHE: This is the specific topic that your blog will be about. You want to try to be as narrow as you can be so that you are attracting your ideal reader.

NO FOLLOW LINK: When you link back to another website, you can decide if it is a no-follow link. This means that it will not help their SEO in any way. No follow links do not count as backlinks but they still count as site visits. This means that you are getting relevant traffic to your site who will likely spend more time on your website.

ON-PAGE SEO: This is the actual content that is on your website. On-page SEO is something that you can control when it comes to your website and your blog.

PAGE TITLE: This is the part of the title that shows up in the search bar when someone goes to that specific page. This is what tells the search engines what your page is about.

PAGE VIEWS: The number of times someone goes to a page on your website.

SEO: Search engine optimization. SEO is how your website will rank on search engines. This is the process of improving your website to increase its organic reach. SEO refers to only organic reach and not paid reach, like ads. It's an algorithm determined by factors that include keyword ranking, backlinks, and page speed.

SHORT-TAIL KEYWORD: These are search terms that are made up of no more than three words.

SSL CERTIFICATE: It is a digital certificate that authenticates a website's identity and enables an encrypted connection. (Source: kaspersky.com) Your website host will be able to provide you with HTTPS security.

SPONSORED POSTS: These are blog posts that bloggers have been paid to write. Sometimes you will also get free products to do these sponsored posts. You can reach out to products/services that you love to see if they would be willing to have you write a sponsored post. It is best if you have a bigger following on social media to do these because they want the post to reach more people. Creating a media kit will help you to easily reach out to companies that you want to work with.

Made in the USA
Monee, IL
03 November 2026

67382579R00046